The Black Out Life Plan:
21 Days to A Healthier Life

Authored by
Alphonso Thomas

The Black Out Life Plan is a motivational guide to not only a healthier diet, but to life inspiration as well. Our mood and state of mind is a direct link to what we eat, how often we exercise as well as to the joy and excitement that we seek in life. Your choice to purchase this book is a direct reflection of your desire for more. Don't fret, you are not alone. You have made a solid choice for help and guidance in your process of new beginnings and I want to personally thank you. Thank you. Your commitment to you is evident and I, too, am committed to helping you accomplish your goals. So, are you ready? Well, LET'S GET STARTED!!

~ Al

Day 1 Detox

A Detox Diet (also called a cleansing diet) will remove toxins and poisons from your body. The idea of a good Detox diet is to eat pure and natural foods that will aid the function of the lymph, kidneys, and liver. All foods that hinder the regime will be avoided. For increased energy, and a way to detoxify a stressed system, set aside a long weekend when you can allow yourself to do very little. While detoxing, it is important to practice meditation where you will begin to develop a deeper understanding of who you are and who you may become. The focus should not be on the length of time or countdown of the days remaining to complete the Black Out Life Plan. Your focus should be enjoying each day of a new way of living. Besides a relaxed state is good for your heart and blood pressure, and your new awareness of breathing and posture will bring increased energy. Meditation will inspire you to find your own creativity and inner resources. You will feel encouraged to get the most benefit out of each day. The Black Out Plan is more than creating meals but more importantly creating the new you.

"Worry invites doubt and blocks creativity"

Brotha Al (UNCUT!!!)

Lemonade Detox

10 oz spring water per day (spread over 6 10 oz glasses)

2 T. Organic Grade B maple syrup

2 T. *freshly squeezed* organic lemon or lime juice (or 2 tbsp. per glass)

1/10 t. cayenne pepper or to taste

Concentrate: Mix together in a dark container equal parts lemon juice and maple syrup. Keep cool until ready to use. Prepare just enough for daily use.

Drink a minimum of at least six to twelve glasses per day. It is best to drink when hunger pangs strike. Always enjoy the master cleanse prepared fresh. On day one after the end of the master cleanse, be careful about what is introduced in your diet. On day one introduce orange juice into your meal plan. On day two introduce vegetable soups and broths and on day three add fruits and vegetables. The first week of this meal plan will follow this guide and days 8-21 will target your goal for improving your life plan.

- Doubt = A distraction that draws forth the thing you don't want and believe you can't have.

+ Meditation = a mental and spiritual exercise that helps you concentrate on receiving the things you want.

The Master Cleanse is an intense detoxification of the body. When you detoxify, you are literally flushing out your glands, organs and colon. You are flushing out chemicals and toxins that your body has accumulated due to poor eating, stress and lack of exercise. A laxative must be taken in the morning and evenings to ensure accumulated wastes are removed. Be sure to observe at least three bowel movements per day.

~ Stanley Burroughs

Stretching & Breathing Model

Detox

At least three times per week you should perform flexibility exercises that use slow movement, deep breathing and involve all major joints of the body. The following are easy and safe options that you can use: (*Side Stretch*) Stand straight up, feet separated to shoulder width, and place your hands on your waist. Now move the upper body to one side and hold the final stretch for a few seconds. Repeat on the other side. (*Lateral Head Tilt*) Tilt the head laterally and repeat several times to each side. (*Arm Circles*) Circle arms all the way around in both directions. Place your arms slightly away from your body and rotate the trunk as far as possible, holding the position for several seconds. Repeat the exercises for both the right and left sides of the body.

(*Shoulder Hyperextension*)Have a partner grasp your arms from behind at the wrist and slowly push them upward. Hold the final position for a few seconds. (*Quad Stretch*) Lie on your side and move one foot back by flexing the knee. Grasp the front of the ankle and pull the ankle toward the gluteal region. Hold the position for several seconds. Repeat with the other leg. (*Heel Cord stretch*) Assume a push –up position, and then bend one knee and stretch the opposite heel cord. Hold the stretched position for a few seconds. Alternate legs. You may also perform the exercise leaning against the wall. (*Adductor Stretch*) Stand with your feet about twice shoulder width and place your hands slightly above the knee. Flex one knee slowly and go down as far as possible, holding the final position for a few seconds. Repeat with the opposite leg. Continue this module and add on a new pose every other day.

A typical herbal Detox will do the following:

~ Dissolve and eliminate toxins that have formed in any part of the body
~ Cleanse kidneys and digestive system
~ Purify the glands and cells
~ Eliminate waste and hardened material in joints and muscles
~ Relieve pressure and irritation in nerves, arteries and blood vessels

Motivation
Meals

Day 2 Foundation

It is said that those responsible for forming a foundation are the Romans. Today, we are going to start by building your foundation for a successfully healthy life plan. LET"S. GET. STARTED! First, we must find the right materials for our project. In this case, it would be the Black Out Life Plan and Journal and a sincere desire for life improvement. Since the day of the Roman Empire many changes for setting the foundation of a building have been tweaked and perfected. From this we know that change for the better is a continuous process. When you walk into your home, do you check the foundation to ensure that it is stable? No, of course you don't. You have an established trust and faith in the foundation of your home and have true confidence that your home is secure. The same must be established within yourself. You must trust that this new foundation you are building upon will not collapse as you face challenges. You must trust that your new foundation will weather the storm and provide all that you need to secure the future you deserve.

Breakfast
½ c. orange juice
½ c. granola
½ c. yogurt

Midmorning Snack
Hand full of almonds

Lunch
Veggie Wrap with Salad
1 whole wheat tortilla
½ of avocado sliced
½ cup of black beans
½ cup pico de gallo
2 cups mixed green salad w/ fresh tangerines

Dinner
6 oz extra firm tofu or veggie steak strips
2 T. Extra Virgin Olive Oil (EVOO)
2 cups of steamed zucchini
1 cup of brown rice

Night Snack
sm./med Plum

- Excuses = serve as justification to remove blame or make apology or grant exemptions; reasons to give up!
+ Drive = people who consistently produce results have discovered a reason that drives them to be more.

Evaluation

Immune System

Before your workout be sure to incorporate stretching and breathing into your routine. To assure a safe performance and evaluation for great results, one should create a Personal Fitness Profile: Pre-Test including cardio respiratory endurance, muscular strength/endurance, flexibility and BMI/body composition. On day 2 briefly state your feelings about your body composition results and your ideal body weight. Do you plan to reduce your percent body weight and increase lean body mass? If so, indicate how you plan to achieve these goals. On day 20 after your work out, re-test to measure your how close you are achieving or even surpassing your goal. It is important not to be frustrated or look at how far you have to go, but focus on what you have accomplished.

Pre-Test	Post-Test

Cardio respiratory Endurance
1.5 Mile Run   Time
_:_
1.0 Mile Walk Time_:_
                Heart Rate_:_
	Cardio respiratory Endurance
	1.5 Mile Run Time _:_
	1.0 Mile Walk Time_:_
	                Heart Rate_:_

Muscular strength/endurance Reps Modified Push-Ups ___ Abs Crunches ___ Overall Fitness Category ___	Muscular strength/endurance Reps Modified Push-Ups ___ Abs Crunches ___ Overall Fitness Category ___
Flexibility Modified Sit-and-Reach Inches	Flexibility Modified Sit-and-Reach Inches ___
BMI/body composition Current body weight ___lbs Current fat percent _ __% Waist seize _ _Inches	BMI/body composition Current body weight ___lbs Current fat percent __% Waist seize __Inches

To ensure that you also get adequate carbohydrate and protein, plan meals to include lentils, wholegrain bread and brown rice, which are also good sources of minerals to boost immune system. While the immune system works to battle a cold or virus, it is likely that other pathogens are trying to invade the body at the same time. The constant threat of infection puts the immune system under tremendous pressure, and we must help it by ensuring that it is supplied with all the nutrients necessary for peak fighting performance. Feeding the "troops" must be the highest priority. The strength (or weakness) of the immune system underlines our biochemical individuality. Someone, whose immune system has been lowered by poor nutrition and immune-suppressors such as sugar and alcohol, may develop the cold, whereas someone with a strong immune system is likely to be relatively unaffected, because the mobilized immune fleet will deal with the infection promptly.

Day 3 Will Power

"Where there is a "Will" there is a way." Easier said than done huh? How does one turn his/her life from average to awesome!! Ask Philadelphia native, Christopher Smith, who grew up amidst the middle class and became one of Hollywood's Elite, earning two Oscar nominations, four Golden Globe nominations and multiple Grammy awards. He is the only actor in history to have eight consecutive films gross over $100 million in the domestic box office, as well as being the only actor to have eight consecutive films in which he starred open at the #1 spot in the domestic box office. Will Smith continues to be an exemplary face for motivation who is quoted saying, "You have to believe that something different will happen." He believes that you don't start to build a wall, without laying a brick every single day. You don't do something because it's mandated or even because you feel it; you do it because you can. By eliminating excuses and procrastination you increase an inner power that is fit to be a contender with success and prepares you for your next stage.

NEXT LEVEL! Let's Get it.

Breakfast
Tropical Energy Blend
1 c. plain yogurt
½ c. pineapple juice
1 banana, frozen and sliced
½ c. frozen orange juice

Midmorning Snack
a handful of toasted pumpkin seeds, almonds, or sunflower seeds

Lunch
2 toasted pieces of whole grain bread, rubbed with olive oil and a bit of garlic
1/2 tablespoon olive oil
1/2 lb of asparagus stalks, trimmed roughly the length of your bread
1 clove garlic, thinly sliced
1/2 teaspoon caraway seeds
1 avocado, pitted and smashed
a couple handfuls of arugula, tossed in a bit of olive oil

Dinner
Chicken and Lettuce Wraps
Hearts of Romaine
8 oz chicken breast or veggie chik'n strips
2 cups of zucchini
½ c. sliced red onion
1 cup of brown rice
2 t. Dijon vinaigrette

Night Snack
Handful of dried cranberries and raw almonds

- Weakness = faint of heart, vulnerable and helpless, fragile or feeble
+ Will =choice to long for, want, hope against hope, show strength of character and self-control

Stretching & Breathing

Add to initial Stretching & Breathing Model from Day Two.

Standing Shoulder Opener - Start your practice with this pose to prepare your arms, shoulders and chest. Stand on your feet, hip-width apart and your leg muscles strong and engaged, quads pulled up, toes spread and lifted. Interlace your fingers behind you, inhale and then lift the sides of your chest so your shoulders are level with the base of your neck. Move the top of your shoulders back with your chin slightly lifted, imagining your shoulder blades connecting to the back of your heart. Exhale; lengthen your arms away from your body and imagine a beam of light shinning out through your heart. Hold for 3 to 5 full, fluid breaths.

Drive (Energy Foods)

If we are looking for energy to continue our new lifestyle it is important to minimize those dietary factors that rob the body of energy or interfere with energy production. These include alcohol, tea, coffee and fizzy drinks, as well as cakes, biscuits and sweets. All such foods stimulate the hormone adrenaline is produced primarily when the body perceives a threat or a challenge to prepare itself for action. It causes the heart to beat faster, the lungs to take in more air, the liver to release extra glucose into the blood, and blood to divert from non-vital areas to where it will be more of use, such as the legs. If adrenaline is constantly over-produced because of stimulant foods, it may lead to general fatigue. There are three different grades of energy food – A, B and C. The A-grade being the most effective.

A-Grade Foods
Complex Carbohydrates
Wholegrain such as oats, barely, brown rice, millet, wholegrain bread, rye bread
Vegetables
Dense vegetables such as broccoli, cauliflower, Brussels sprouts, mushrooms, turnips, carrots (especially raw), asparagus, artichokes, spinach
Fruit
Avocado, apple, pear, pineapple, berries-Strawberries, raspberries, blackberries, cherries
Protein
Salmon, tuna, herring, mackerel, seaweeds, eggs, tofu, walnuts, brazil nuts, sunflower seeds, pumpkin seeds, sesame seeds, linseeds. Sprouted seeds and grains, haricot and lima beans, chick peas, lentils and soya beans

Day 4 Champion

Your mission: Elevate from contender to champion. This is to prove that your accomplishments are not a hoax, but something you can very easily do again. It's only day 4, but you are here and that says a lot about your drive to champion your new life plan. Unlike many of us when we are faced with a difficult obstacle, we simply throw in the towel. Instead, you are facing your strong holds and knocking them out one by one; like an opponent soon to be destroyed. Let's look at a young man, Iron Mike Tyson, who had an appetite for destruction that led to unparalleled success. At the age of 20, he broke records as the youngest heavyweight champion in history while also becoming the first in his weight class to hold three major belts. Iron Mike's career seem to take a nose dive after being defeated by an unknown Buster Douglas; however, recognize that champions are not measured by losing a tough duel, but by winning multiple duels. Remember we all have set backs, but a true champion may lose a battle, but never their legacy that is his/her true title. Iron Mike Tyson opponents feared his knockout punches as your strong holds should fear the champion inside of you. *WINNING!*

"It is impossible to be defeated when one never gives up"
     ~ Brotha Al (UNCUT!!!)

Breakfast
Energy Shake
1 ½ c. fresh orange juice
1 banana, frozen, peeled, cut into 2 inch chunks
½ c. coarsely chopped kale leaves, center stalk removed
½ kiwi, peeled
2 pitted dates, coarsely chopped

Midmorning Snack
A slice of Cantaloupe

Lunch
Chicken Lettuce Wraps
Hearts of Romaine
4 oz. boneless chicken breast
1/4 cup low fat, plain or sugar-free yogurt
1/4 tsp. curry powder
1/2 cup red or green grapes, halved

Dinner
Grilled Tilapia with Fennel- Mint Tzatziki
½ cup of finely diced fennel bulb
½ cup Greek style yogurt
¾ T chopped fresh mint
½ t white balsamic vinegar
2 T extra virgin olive oil (EVOO)
2 large tilapia fillets
½ t fennel seeds, finely ground
1 cup of Broccoli with lemon and 1 T. olive oil

Night Snack
½ cup of Tropical Fruit Salad

- Fear = the acceptance of defeat
+ Ambition = strong desire to achieve something

Cardio/Workout

Addiction

Now that you have your Personal Fitness Profile Pre-Test completed and you have created a plan for maximizing your potentials. You can begin to incorporate 30 to 60 minutes of moderate intensity physical activity at least three days out of a week. If your schedule does not allow you to work out on the days suggested, create one that what works best for you. Be creative by naming the days of your schedule, making it more fun and personal.

OWN YOUR DAY!!!

My Daily Examples:

Intense Tuesday:
Take your work out to another level by adding weights or increasing reps, inclines or full resistance in all areas.

Freight Train Friday:
Explore your maximum drive by increasing your heart rate with unstoppable force. Push yourself, but be cautious. Freight Train Fridays will allow you to gradually increase your workout pace Monday-Thursday.

Different substances deplete the body of different nutrients. Including alcohol, over-the-counter drugs and caffeine. For example, the body recognizes alcohol as a poison. Some of the effects of chronic alcohol consumption include damage to the brain, liver, pancreas, duodenum, and central nervous system. Alcoholism causes metabolic damage to every cell in the body and depresses the immune system. It may take years before the consequences of excessive drinking become evident, but if an alcoholic continues to drink; his and her life span may be shortened by ten to fifteen years or more. Alcohol is broken down in the liver and the continuous consumption of alcohol inhibits its production of digestive enzymes, impairing the body's ability to absorb proteins, fats, and the fat-soluble vitamins (vitamins A, D, E, and K), as well as B-complex vitamins (especially thiamine and folic acid) and other water-soluble vitamins.

Whatever your addiction, be cautious, speak with your family doctor or other physician, and commit to incorporating the necessary changes to help you overcome this stronghold. The goal of the Black Out Life Plan is to help you through the process of creating a life plan that makes living this life more valuable to you, more rewarding, more fulfilling, much healthier, and even more exciting. Take time to learn about your addiction and the affects that it has on your health and wellness.

Motivation	Meal

Day 5 Change

(GBO Adult Education) "In nature, change continually takes place; some changes are hardly noticeable, such as water evaporating from a lake. Some changes are welcome, such as a baby getting older. Some changes are not welcome, such as a car rusting. But, change welcome or not is a daily part of our lives, even when we are not it remains consistent." Consistency is what developed a young girl from India, who was unable to afford a business suit for her interview into one of Wall Street Journal's list of 50 women to watch in 2007 and 2008, one of Time Magazine's 100 most influential people in the world, as well as Forbes most powerful women in 2008. Indra Nooyiin was named President and CFO of PepsiCo in 2001. See Indra, as well as the Black Out Life Plan acknowledge that before change can take place in one's diet, self or the world; he must first change his mindset so he can overcome debilitating habits. Take today to identify changes that you hope to make during this process and commit daily to "becoming the change that you wish to see." Ghandi says it best in that if you want to see change in your life, your body composition, or your health, then you will have to become that change first.

~ Make That Change!

Breakfast
Cinnamon Buckwheat Pancakes
4 Teaspoons Pure Maple Syrup

Midmorning Snack
½ cup Spanish Trail Mix
2 cups whole natural almonds
1 ½ t smoked paprika
1 t finely grated orange peel
1 cup cubed dried apricots
1 cup cubed pitted dates
¼ cup dark chocolate chunks
Cayenne to taste

Lunch
Raw Mustard Greens Salad with Toasted Sunflower Seeds and Grilled Chicken
½ c up Sunflower Seeds (oven toasted)
1 bunch mustard greens, center rib and stem cut and leaves cut crosswise
5 teaspoons lemon juice
4 oz. Grilled chicken breast

Dinner
Stir Fried Bok Choy and Arugula and Tofu
3 ½ T soy sauce
4 t Asian sesame oil
3 ½ t unseasoned rice vinegar
1 container extra firm tofu, drained
2 T peanut oil
1 T finely chopped, peeled ginger
2 garlic cloves chopped
4 baby bok choy, leaves separated
6 cups of arugula

Night Snack
Frozen banana with 1 T. peanut butter

- Failure = Measuring our outcomes without continuing

+ Consistency = Uncountable attempts to succeed

Stretching & Breathing

Add to Stretching & Breathing Model

Standing forward bend: This pose stretches your chest, shoulders and hamstrings. It also helps curb fatigue and anxiety. From the Standing Shoulder Opener inhale and engage your leg muscles, then exhale and bow forward from your hips, bending your knees slightly. As your arms lengthen over the back of your body, lift your shoulder blades as if you connecting them with the base of your heart. Continue to stretch your shoulders backward, feeling the space being created in and around your heart. Hold for 3 to 5 slow and steady breaths.

The Health Benefits of Tea

Instead of soda and other fruit drinks, try a soothing beverage that is packed with protective antioxidants. Tea is the second most popular drink in the world (water is the top choice). Although most people think of tea as a soothing and delicious beverage, it possesses a remarkable wealth of antioxidants. All teas, whether black, green, oolong or white, are harvested from the leaves of a variety of plant known as the camellia sinensis. The primary distinction between the different teas is the amount of fermentation they undergo. Black teas are the most fermented, white teas the least. Both black coffee and unsweetened teas contain no sugar or starches. However, adding additional flavoring can greatly increase the calorie count and sugar/starch content of the drink. To limit the calorie content, do not add sugar, sweetened creamers, whipped cream or other flavorings to your coffee or tea.

~All true teas contain polyphones, powerful antioxidants believed to protect against heart disease, certain cancers and stroke.

~ The various levels of fermentation affect teas in different ways. Recent studies have shown drinking green tea might boost metabolism, oolong teas can lower blood sugar, and black teas can promote oral health.

Tea contains half the caffeine of coffee.

Day 6 Pledge

In 1892 Congress looked for United States to have an oath of loyalty to the national flag. What they found was a Baptist Ministers inoculation that would protect immigrants and the native born from radicalism and subversion. In the September issue of a popular children's magazine, the Youth's Comparison to the Pledge of Allegiance was Born by Francis Bellamy. Today all Americans protect their hearts with their right hand and pledge, "One nation under God." A pledge is not just reciting words, rather it is a commitment to a verbal contract that you agree to uphold and live by.

Day 6 Pre-Activity Plan

Create seven principles to live by. These principles should be for self. These principles should coincide with your character and personal beliefs. No matter what challenges or temptations you come across, make a pledge to uphold the principles with which your character and everyday beliefs are aligned.

Example:
1. Honor and give praise to the power within
2. Respect the divine order and expect a greater return
3. Be the author to what you give meaning to
4. Always take action never react
5. Be selective and precise in what strengths you use
6. Develop wisdom adequate to govern the world
7. Never waiver principles

Breakfast
Energy Shake
1 ½ c. fresh orange juice
1 banana, frozen, peeled, cut into 2 inch chunks
½ c. coarsely chopped kale leaves, center stalk removed
½ kiwi, peeled
2 pitted dates, coarsely chopped

Midmorning Snack
1 cup of blueberries, strawberries, and raspberries with 1 t honey drizzled

Lunch
Bunch of arugula
4 oz lean steak, grilled/broiled
8 oz Spiral sliced zucchini
Caesar Dressing
2 oz feta cheese

Dinner
Spicy Shrimp Quesadillas
   12 large shrimp, grilled and coarsely chopped
   2 T chopped fresh cilantro + additional for garnish
   3 jalapenos, seeded and thinly sliced
   2 T chopped shallot
   1 T fresh lime juice
   2 c coarsely grated Jack cheese
   8 7 to 8 inch whole wheat tortillas
   8 teaspoons EVOO

Night Snack
Handful of Granola and raisins

- **Attempt** = Expectation of limitation

+ **Commitment** = Undeniable effort

Cardio/Workout

*Basic Workout module
(see all images on p. 13)*

Prone Bridge
Starting in prone position on a floor mat, balance yourself on the tips of your toes and elbows while attempting to maintain a straight body from heels to toes (do not arch your back) After awhile you can increase the difficulty of the exercise by placing your hands in front of you and straightening the arms. Time yourself and hold position for 1 minute for beginners increasing to 3 minutes as your strength increases.

Abdominal Crunch and Bent-Leg Curl-Up
Start with your head and shoulders off the floor, arms crossed on your chest, and knees slightly bent. Now curl up to about a 30 degrees angle, and then return to the straight position without letting your head or shoulders touch the floor.

Add 3 more abdominal exercises from circuit training.
Push-Up
Maintaining your body as straight as possible, flex the elbows, lowering the body until you almost touch the floor, then raise yourself back up to the starting position. If you are unable to perform the push-up as instructed, you can decrease the resistance by supporting the lower body with the knees rather than the feet.

Add 3 more upper body exercises from circuit training.

The Health Benefits of Nuts and Seeds

Incorporate a handful of these crunchy snacks into your diet.
Although high in calories, nuts often enable people to maintain or lose weight. A small handful eaten between meals or added to salads, grains or vegetables gives a sense of satiety and results in less total food intake. Nuts have great nutritional benefits, as well.

> *Almonds, pecans and pistachios are rich in protein.*
>
> *Walnuts contain omega-3 fatty acids.*
>
> *Toss sesame seeds in a meal for extra calcium and vitamin E.*
>
> *Sesame, sunflower and pumpkin seeds are particularly good sources of phytosterols, also known as plant sterols, which promote heart health.*

Since nuts are high in fats, they can easily become rancid. Store them in the freezer to extend their life. Nuts are also delicious, so it's also a good idea to practice portion control. Measure out small portions and take care to not eat them mindlessly from a large container.

PRONE BRIDGE

ABDOMINAL CRUNCH

PUSH UP

Day 7 Perception

Human beings have a tendency to perceive things the way they want; however, an individual's perception is based on what their life has shown them. Do we call the lioness who hunts for food to feed her cubs a murderer or provider? If the influences from society's perception is in charge of directing our path, then Ted Ross says, "We are incapable of being king." For example, after being discharged from US Air force he continued his career in show business and is well known for his role in 1978 film The Wiz as the cowardly lion. Like the cowardly lion, some of us are living out roles that have strayed off course because of the influence of fear and our perceptions. We wonder why our journey has been prolonged or why we haven't quite arrived to our destination. It is because our brain is designed to only go forward on what we perceive to be true, making us incapable to receive because we fail to believe. Today, I charge you to change the perception of your life, your health, your career, your family and anything else that is off course. Start believing that what you truly want to have is yours and it will be just that...YOURS!

~ You have completed your first week! At the end of the book are pages for you to write your reflections for each week that you complete. Talk about how you feel, your energy levels, and add a picture if you like.

Breakfast
1 egg or 2 oz egg substitute
1/2 cup cooked oatmeal
1 Cup Milk
1 oz raisins
1/2 diced apple
Drizzle of Honey

Midmorning Snack
Handful of Raw Almonds

Lunch
4 ½ oz. salmon fillet
¼ t. lemon pepper seasoning
½ cup of brown rice
3 T. cooked lentils
¼ t. onion powder
¼ t. cumin
1 T. fresh parsley

Dinner
Grilled Open Face Eggplant and Smoked Gouda
1 lb. Tomatoes, finely chopped
¼ c. finely chopped fresh flat leaf parsley
½ c plus 2 T. EVOO
1 T. white wine vinegar
½ t. black pepper
1 t. Kosher Salt
1- 8 oz. Piece smoked cheese (gouda)
4 slices whole grain bread
2-1 lb. Eggplants

Night Snack
Tropical Fruit Salad – 1 cup serving
1 c. diced peeled pitted mango
1 c. diced peeled, cored pineapple
1 c. diced peeled bananas
2 T. pure maple syrup

- **Coward** = Fear of what is unknown or proven
+ **Bravery** = to face incoming or existing troubles

Stretching & Breathing

Add to Stretching & Breathing Model

Downward-Facing Dog - This pose opens your back and heart center, creates suppleness in your spine and helps you feel the full length and strength of your body. Come to all fours, with hands shoulder-width apart and knees hip-width apart. Keeping your arms strong, feel as if you are melting your heart toward the mat as you draw your shoulder blades down your back. As you inhale, curl your toes under; lift your hips and stretch your thighs back, keeping your leg muscles strong. Exhale and press your heels towards the mat. Engage the muscles of your arms and legs and root your hands and feet firmly into the mat. Keeping your hips up and your thighs back, allow your heart to expand. Let a feeling of openness permeate your entire body. Hold for 3 to 5 complete breaths.

The Health Benefits of Salmon

All fish are great sources of protein and low in saturated fat. But cold-water fish, like salmon, mackerel and herring, are premiere sources of omega-3 essential fatty acids. These are fats our bodies can't produce, so it's essential we include them in our diet. Omega-3s offer many benefits. Salmon is an easy fish to obtain. Most grocery stores and many restaurants carry it. It's also easy to cook. The high fat level makes salmon perfect for grilling, roasting or sautéing without sticking or drying out. Although wild salmon can be pricey, it has an amazing flavor and higher levels of omega-3s than farm-raised fish. Look for fresh wild salmon in spring and summer, and farm-raised salmon year-round.

~ They reduce the risk of heart disease and cancer.

~ They minimize the symptoms of arthritis and inflammatory diseases.

~ They contribute to healthy skin and hair.

~ They may help with depression.

Day 8 Visualization

"What you see is what you get," True or Not True? It is said that blind people dream just like sighted people do, but don't see in their dreams because they have no visual images to base their dreams on. This never stopped super stars Ray Charles, who began to lose his sight at 5 and Stevie Wonder who was blind shortly after birth. A vision strong enough is unlikely to be delayed due to short comings. Ask the seventeen year old from New York who borrowed one thousand dollars from friends to open his first sandwich shop on August 28, 1965. He worked at a low wage paying job at a hardware store while trying to raise money to pay for college. He was co-founder of one of the biggest franchises in history beating out even *McDonalds* as the number one restaurant chain. Visualization helps us to be more descriptive in thought. The more precise our image the more real it is.

Day 8 Activity

It is true; some of us are more kinesthetic, while others are more visual. This activity will allow our minds to focus more on what we desire by literally painting a picture where we want to see ourselves. Cut out images from magazines or newspaper ads on what you desire to acquire. If you get a chance test drive the car you want or visit an open house on the market. Take in the smell and feel the surface so that your senses record it for next time you are visualizing, preferably during meditation.

"If you can dream it, you can become or have it!"

Breakfast
½ c. Dried Cranberries
Large Sweet Apple (I use Fuji)
1 c. Oatmeal
1 t. brown sugar

Midmorning Snack
1 c. Tropical Fruit Salad (from day 6)

Lunch
Mixed Greens with Pears, Walnuts, Gorgonzola and Green Tea Vinaigrette
2 T. Champagne vinegar
1 T. minced shallot
1 T. chopped fresh chives
2 t. Dijon mustard
1 t. dried basil
1 t. matcha green-tea powder
6 T. EVOO
6 c. loosely packed mixed greens
2 pears, peeled, halved lengthwise, cut into ½ inch wedges
½ c. crumbled Gorgonzola cheese

Dinner
Sweet & Sour Chicken
1 lb. skinless, boneless chicken breasts, cut into strips
1 Tbsp. minced fresh ginger
1-2 Tbsp. lite soy sauce (optional)
2 cups red bell pepper strips
1 cup green onions, sliced in 1-inch pieces
3/4 cup fat-free chicken broth
1 Tbsp. cornstarch
1 can (11 oz.) mandarin oranges, drained
1 can (8 oz.) sliced water chestnuts, drained
½ c brown rice
1 c steamed broccoli

Night Snack
1 banana with 1 T. peanut butter

- Pessimistic = Worrying about what could possibly go wrong by focusing on the things that we don't have as a handicap

+ Optimistic = Making lemonade out of lemons, capturing every moment and every possibility as an opportunity

Cardio/Workout

Basic Workout Module plus 3 circuit training activities for upper body, abdominal and lower body.

Circuit training is short bursts of resistance exercise using moderate weights and frequent repetitions, followed quickly by another burst of exercise targeting a different muscle group.
Because you switch between muscle groups, no rest is needed between exercises. This gets the heart rate up, which usually doesn't happen during resistance exercise. Sometimes, to increase heart rate further, aerobics are sprinkled between the resistance exercises.

Upper Body	Abdominal	Lower Body
All upper body exercises require 3 max reps in 1minute	You can effectively work your abs with 3 non-consecutive workouts a week	Some exercises may require leg machines - or repeat lunges with weights
Bench press or pushups	Crunch and Reach	Squats
Pull-ups or Pull downs	Reverse Crunch	Bike or jog 3 minutes
Military press	Bicycle	Lunges 1:00 min each leg
Bicep curls	Wood Chops	Leg ext 1:00 minute
Triceps extensions	Knee Tucks	Leg curls 1:00 minute

Like all other parts of the body, the eyes need to be nourished properly. In addition to making sure that the eyes are not strained by intense close work or inadequate light, proper eye care includes a healthy diet containing sufficient amounts of vitamins and minerals. In order to promote good eyesight, you must make sure your diet contains the proper amounts of the b vitamins, vitamins A, C, and E, and the minerals selenium and zinc. Fresh fruits and vegetables are good sources of these vitamins and minerals. It's best to include plenty of these in your diet, especially yellow and yellow-orange foods such as carrots, yams, and cantaloupes. A well balanced diet with plenty of fresh fruits and vegetables can help keep your eyes healthy, so stock your fridge with a rainbow of vegetables and foods.

Orange and yellow-hued veggies like winter squash, carrots and sweet potatoes and leafy greens contain carotenoids, a pigment our body converts to vitamin A. Eating lots of these vegetables will help maintain healthy skin and hair, protect against prostate cancer, promote healthy vision and even provide protection from sunburn.

Although garlic and onions may lack the vibrant colors of other vegetables, they contain daily sulfide and saponins, compounds that add distinctive flavors to our recipes and fight cancer and heart disease.

Day 9 Longevity

Developing a healthy life style is not a fly by night venture. The Black Out Life Plan is not a diet. Most diets offer temporary solutions to lifelong concerns. We do not refer to this plan as a diet to eliminate confusion; We are not expecting you to adopt the Black Out Life Plan into your life just to shave off a couple of pounds only to impress a high school reunion class. The hope is to increase your drive and motivation for healthier living while decreasing stress related thinking about long term health issues. Take Maria Gomes Valentim, the oldest person in the world who dies in Brazil at 115 on her birthday. Guinness says that Valentim, known as Grandma Quilta attributed her longevity to a healthy diet. We may esteem our elders in a eulogy by saying "he or she lived a long life," but living a long life is more than acquiring age. It is an unselfish responsibility that gives wisdom to younger spectators. The longer you live, the more wisdom and knowledge you acquire thus enabling you to impart this wisdom on generations to come. This wisdom is what has been passed down to help build kingdoms, religions, and cultural practices that provide a richer and better world. Living your life with health issues or chronic illnesses that could have been prevented is not just critical for you, but is a disservice to the generations after you. Today, be healed. *Live your long life with richness, promise, and a goal for change.*

Breakfast
½ c. of Dried Blueberries
1 banana
1 cup oat meal

Midmorning Snack
Slices of 1 orange and a handful of raw almonds

Lunch
Grilled Shrimp, Lettuce, and Cherry Tomato Salad with Aioli Dressing
5 oz. Blackened shrimp
12 cups torn romaine lettuce from 1 large head
8 oz cherry tomatoes
1 garlic clove, pressed
3 T. plain yogurt/veganaise
1 ½ T. white wine vinegar

Dinner
Blackened Shrimp over Tropical Pico de Gallo
See index for Recipe

Night Snack
½ cup strawberry sorbet

- **Anxious** = Rushing your process looking for Quick fix results
+ **Patience** = Learning to appreciate gradual growth and not getting caught up in the moment, but accepting a long-term lifestyle.

Stretching & Breathing

Add to Stretching & Breathing Model

Locust - This powerful shoulder opener helps engage and strengthen the muscles of your back in order to support the opening of the chest. Lie on your belly and clasp your hands behind your back. On an inhalation, lengthen your upper body forward and lift your chest and heart off the mat without raising your legs. Exhale and scoop your tailbone under, engage your belly, and extend out through your legs as you lift your arms up and behind you. Continue to lengthen the sides of your body as you keep your shoulder blades rooted on your back, and shine out through your heart. Breathe deeply and hold for 3 to 5 complete breaths.

The Health Benefits of Legumes

The inexpensive legume family, which includes beans, peas, peanuts and lentils, has priceless benefits and adds longevity to life. Best of all, beans taste great. Dried beans have a superior taste and texture but they take longer to cook. Canned beans offer a quick alternative and most of the same health benefits. Rinse canned beans with water before cooking and you'll remove as much as 40 percent of the sodium used in processing.

Legumes are rich in folic acid, calcium, iron, potassium, zinc and antioxidants.

Their high protein and complex carbohydrates provide steady energy that lasts for hours.

They are especially high in soluble fiber, and a daily serving of cooked beans may lower blood cholesterol by as much as 18 percent, decreasing the risk of heart disease.

Most legumes also contain protease inhibitors, compounds thought to suppress cancer cells and slow tumor growth.

Day 10 - Challenges

Challenges will show up at your doorstep the second you make a commitment. Your goals will neither be easy, nor attainable with an effortless attempt. You have to want it! In life, if you are expecting growth, then you must also anticipate the challenges that come with it. The Black Out Plan is unbiased in that when it comes to providing a framework for creating a healthier lifestyle we show our hand. We don't paint the picture that you will be all smiles during the process. You will face challenges. You will want to quit. But, HOW BAD DO YOU WANT IT? You're half way through it and have accomplished so much already. Seriously, you're ready to give that up TODAY? No, you're not!!! Do you want it bad enough to continue and press through the struggle? Yes, you do, **SO LET"S GO GET IT!!!** The Black Out Life Plan anticipates these challenges, especially when it comes to the lack of motivation. That's why the stories posted offer real life experiences instead of theories and speculation. The Black Out Life Plan realizes that you are much stronger than the challenges in front of you.

Gail Devers stunned the world of track and field by bouncing back from a severe illness to win the gold medal in the 100 meter sprint at the 1992 Olympic Games in Barcelona, Spain. Gail understood that challenges are a merely decoys that cannot stop you from pursuing your goal.

GO GET IT! I said, "GO GET IT!!!!!

Breakfast
Berry Energy Shake
1 banana, frozen, peeled, and sliced
½ cup fresh or frozen blackberries
½ cup fresh or frozen blueberries
2 packets Stevia Extract In The Raw
½ cup light vanilla soymilk or almond milk

Midmorning Snack
1 medium apple and 1 T. peanut butter

Lunch
Tuna Wraps
1 T olive oil
2 medium plum tomatoes, seeded, finely chopped
1 medium onion, finely chopped
2 garlic cloves
1 pound high quality tuna packed in olive oil
2 large hard boiled eggs, peeled, sliced
1 pkg. whole wheat flat bread
Lettuce of choice

Dinner
Glazed Salmon
2 T. olive oil, plus more for brushing
4 tablespoons light soy sauce
Juice of 2 lemons
½ onion, finely chopped
2 tablespoons packed light brown sugar
2 cloves garlic, minced
1 teaspoon toasted sesame oil
Freshly ground pepper
4 5-to-6-ounce wild salmon filet, skin removed
½ cup of wild and brown rice
1 cup sautéed spinach with olive oil and garlic

Night Snack
½ cup of granola with ¼ cup dried cranberries

- **Limitations** = Road blocks, setbacks, timelines are all related when telling ourselves this is good enough, I didn't expect to get this far. I should stop while I'm ahead.
+ **Expectations** = Eliminate restrictions which narrow your range. Open up the gates of possibility. Expect greatness daily as a part of your life.

Cardio/Workout

Vitamins and Minerals

Repeat Basic work out w/ circuit training

Knee Tucks -Start in plank position on the ball, with the ball under the shins/ankles. Roll the ball towards you with your feet, tightening the abs into a crunch.

Biceps

Lunges

Eating certain vitamins and minerals like folic acid and B vitamins can help keep your mood steady because they're needed to make serotonin, which is a chemical that directly affects mood in a positive way." As with vitamins, it can be difficult, if not impossible, to obtain the amounts of minerals needed for optimum health through diet alone. Mineral supplements can help to make sure you are getting all the minerals your body requires. Minerals are often found in multivitamin formulas. Minerals can also be sold as single supplements. These are available in tablet, capsule, powder, and liquid forms. Some are available in chelated form, which means that the minerals are bonded to protein molecules that transport them to the blood stream and enhance their absorption. When mineral supplements are taken with a meal, they are usually automatically chelated in the stomach during digestion. There is some controversy over which mineral supplements are best; the various chelated formulas available have shown that, in general, orotate and arginate forms of minerals make the most effective supplements.

Motivation	Meal Plan

Day 11 Duty

Work and Duty is as different as day and night. Most of us work to survive or maintain a certain lifestyle. Duty is more of a responsibility that is not motivated by wager or amount, but principle. John Henry is an American folk hero, notable for having raced against a steam powered hammer and won. In his effort to challenge machinery as an attempt to arrest job reduction, he proved that he was just as if not more capable to perform the job. There was neither reward nor wager for his victory. It was not his job, but his duty to accomplish this task. Many of us have grown accustom to only being motivated by material return instead of internal return. The Dictionary describes Duty as something that one is expected or required to do by moral or legal obligation. A moral commitment is the sort that results in action and is not a matter of positive feeling or mere recognition. Duty does involve some sacrifice of immediate self-interest. You should not look at gym or diet as work, but as an assignment to maintain and improve your health. It's your duty!

Work Ethic System

The work ethic reflects the belief that work is good in itself and that success results from hard work.

Buchholz,1978

Breakfast
1 egg or 2 oz egg substitute
1 cup cooked couscous
2 oz golden raisins
1 diced apple (granny smith)
Drizzle of Honey (orange blossom is yummy!)
(save ½ cup for lunch)

Midmorning Snack
1 large banana and handful of almonds or 1/2 cup of almond milk with a sprinkle of cinnamon.

Lunch
Indian Eggplant and Onion Dip w/ Pita Chips
3 whole wheat pita rounds cut in wedges
4 T. olive oil, divided
1 1 ¼ lb eggplant, quartered lengthwise
2 ½ c chopped onions
2 unpeeled garlic cloves
2 T. chopped fresh mint
2 T. fresh cilantro
½ t garam masala

Dinner
Grilled Chicken Breast w/ Orange Pineapple Chutney
4 boneless/skinless chicken breast or thighs
1 ½ navel oranges
1 golden delicious apple, peeled, cored, cubed
½ red onion, coarsely chopped
1/3 cup fresh cilantro
1 T chopped/seeded jalapeno
1 T evoo
1 T red wine vinegar
1 T agave nectar/honey (orange blossom is great!)
1 t of garam masala
1 t minced peeled fresh ginger
Serve with ½ cup of brown rice per serving

Night Snack
½ cup of granola with ¼ cup dried cranberries

- **Labor** = When one's motive to produce is only to survive, it can only be viewed as work.
+ **Worth** = An unselfish gesture that will benefit you and others

Stretching & Breathing

Add to Stretching & Breathing Model

Low Lunge (Feb 2010 Natural Health Magazine) This hip and heart opener enables you to stretch more deeply than other lunges allow because your back knee and front foot ground you. Standing tall and strong on the mat, step your right foot forward and gently place your back knee on the mat. If you find it tough to balance at first, keep your back toes curled under for support. Scoop your tailbone and circle your arms upward. Draw your shoulder blades farther down your back, and let that motion help you open your heart skyward. Keep both legs strong and engaged as you hold the pose for 3 to 5 full breaths. Switch legs and repeat.

The Health Benefits of Lean Proteins

Modest portions of these meat and dairy products will fill you up without adding to your waistline

Protein is an important part of every diet and is found in many different foods. Lean protein, the best kind, can be found in fish, skinless chicken and turkey, pork tenderloin and certain cuts of beef, like the top round. Low-fat dairy products like milk, yogurt, ricotta and other cheeses supply both protein and calcium.

Protein is crucial for tissue repair, building and preserving muscle, and making important enzymes and hormones.

Lean meats and dairy contribute valuable minerals like calcium, iron, selenium and zinc. These are not only essential for building bones, and forming and maintaining nerve function, but also for fighting cancer, forming blood cells and keeping immune systems robust.

Day 12 Transition

In one of 70's popular shows, David Banner turns unto Incredible Hulk, the inner green giant with unhuman strength, played by Lou Ferringo. But, in real life Ferringo had to also tap into an inner strength that was greater than a severe ear infection which resulted in partial but permanent hearing loss. He went on in spite of doubters to become the youngest body builder ever to win Mr. Universe. Lou Ferringo quoted, "If I hadn't lost my hearing, I wouldn't be where I am now. It forced me to maximize my potential. I had to be better than the average person to succeed." Like the Hulk many of us have another person inside of us whom we are often afraid of the triggers that awaken the beast within. Mainly because we believe it will take over. In the 2012 Avengers, Dr. Banner had claimed to manage his temper with new techniques, but when trouble surfaces the beast is quickened still. A successful transition is not running from the more aggressive you, but realizing that it is in you and at all times, you are in control of it! You also control the past that you have brought with you. At times if you catch yourself stuck in transition, it is because the beast in you is trying to resolve a conflict or situation that is foreign to its understanding. Trust me; there will be times when the Beast is needed, like when going the extra mile on a run or maxing out the last rep before finishing your set. So, come on. **Unleash the Beast!!** Your transition requires being comfortable with who you've become and how well you adjust.

Breakfast
Energy Shake
1 ½ c. fresh orange juice
1 banana, frozen, peeled, cut into 2 inch chunks
½ c. coarsely chopped kale leaves, center stalk removed
½ kiwi, peeled
2 pitted dates, coarsely chopped

Midmorning Snack
a handful of toasted pepitas, or almonds, or sunflower seeds and small slice of cantaloupe

Lunch
Beet and Tangerine Salad w/ Cranberry Dressing
3- 2 ½ in diameter red beets, tops trimmed
3 large tangerines
3 T. evoo
3 T. frozen cranberry juice cocktail, thawed
1 T raspberry vinegar
1/3 c paper thin slices red onion
1 large bunch watercress, thick stems trimmed
1 boneless skinless chicken breast, grilled, sliced

Dinner
Tomato, Fennel, and Crab Soup
¼ c olive oil
3 ½ c chopped onions
2 med fennel bulbs w/ fronds cored, sliced
3 large garlic cloves, minced
2 -14 ½ oz. Diced tomatoes in juice
2 c vegetable broth
8 oz. Crab meat
4 thick slices rustic whole wheat (grain) bread

Night Snack
½ c strawberry sorbet with ½ c. fresh blueberries

- Mediocrity = To accept a lower level of living

+ Maximize = To impact your greatest potential

Cardio/Workout

Repeat Basic work out w/ circuit training

Wood chop - Attach one end of a resistanc band to something sturdy and wrap the ban around your hand a few times for the righ tension. Grasp the band in both hands an begin in a lunge position, reaching dow with the arms. Keeping the arms straight th entire time, rotate and lift the body toward the other side while sweeping the arms on diagonal. Return to start and repeat befor moving onto the other side.

Pull Ups

Leg Extension

Lean and Green

Avocados

These green guys are chock full of antioxidants and heart healthy fats - including saturated fats that help support the production of testosterone, the hormone you need to produce muscle. Avocados pretty much rule since they taste great on just about anything.

Broccoli

This cruciferous veggie is nearly 40% protein and high in fiber and low in calories making it an awesome way to get a lot of nutrition out of food that's easy on the waistline. I enjoy dipping raw broccoli in hummus as a snack.

Spinach

It generally goes without saying but green leafy veggies probably have the most concentrated nutrition of any food you can find. Replace lettuce in your salads and sandwiches with spinach and you'll be adding extra protein, iron and fiber to your diet. Another nutrient-dense stalwart in the green leafy veggie family, eating collard greens is like taking a potent multivitamin: They're packed with vitamins A, B, C, E, and K, as well as Foliate. Try them as wraps for your favorite sandwiches

Green vegetables like broccoli and spinach are sky-high in potent anti-cancer compounds like sulforaphane and quercitin.

Motivation

Day 13 - Healthy Distractions

The key to accomplishing ones goal is determined by their thinking. Sometimes in order to escape our surroundings, we must off set our mind of absorbing unwanted temptations by staying occupied. But, if we never see the door to the way out, how can we escape? What will stop a prisoner from just walking out the front door? There are two reasons that deter his thought. One, he has never seen the door, so he may need assistance getting there from an outside resource, particularly someone who has seen the way out. The second would be the guards who would definitely stop him from even considering the thought. For those who have countered a master mind escape often rely on a diversion. The same thing you will need to do, if you wish to complete The Black Out Life Plan: 21 days to a complete lifestyle makeover. I'm sure we all remember Tommy "Tiny" Lister Jr., the 6'5 275 pound actor better known as Debo. He was a character in Ice Cubes' Hit comedy Friday. As a young student, he threw a shot put to stay out of harm's way in Compton, Los Angeles; breaking the school record seven times in one year, his longest distance was 63 feet at Cal State, who hosts a track meet every year called the Tommy "Tiny" Lister Classic.

Day 13 Activity

Choose an exercise or activity that preoccupies the mind. Take up a short course of knitting or venture off in fishing, something relaxing and not complex that will create frustration.

Meal Plan

Breakfast
Mushroom & Spinach Frittata with Roasted Tomatoes
1-10.5 oz container grape tomatoes
¾ c diced shallots, divided
1 t. evoo
12 oz. Mushrooms (crimini/stemmed shitake), diced
1 c fresh baby spinach, wilted
2 ½ T chopped fresh basil, divided
6 large eggs
1 T Dijon mustard
1/3 c crumbled fresh goat cheese
Splash of balsamic vinegar

Midmorning Snack
Handful of almonds and dried cranberries

Lunch
Grilled Hearts of Romaine with blue Cheese vinaigrette and pickled onions
1 ¾ c white wine vinegar, divided
½ c. sugar
½ c water
3 Turkish bay leaves
½ t crushed red pepper
1 to 1 ¼ lbs red onions sliced thinly
½ t Dijon mustard
½ c olive oil
½ c crumbled blue cheese
4 hearts of romaine, quartered
Crumbled blue cheese, for garnish

Dinner
Salmon Burgers
5 whole grain buns
12 oz skinless, boneless salmon fillets
3 green onions
1 egg
1 t. seafood seasoning
3 oz smoked salmon, hot style
1 T. olive oil
1/3 c light mayonnaise/veganaise
Cucumber, green onions, lemons

Night Snack
½ c strawberry sorbet with ½ c. fresh blueberries

- **Avoid** = Hide or give in to unwanted attraction
+ **Conquer** = Persistence upon one's quest

Stretching & Breathing

The Health Benefits of Olive Oil

Add to Stretching & Breathing Model

Hip Flexors Stretch - Kneel down on an exercise mat, a soft surface, or place a towel under your knees. Raise the left knee off the floor and place the left foot about 3 feet in front of you. Place your left hand over your left knee and the right hand over the back of the hip. Keeping the lower back flat, slowly move forward and downward as you apply gentle pressure over the right hip. Repeat the exercise with the opposite leg forward.

Olive oil is a staple in any kitchen. It's the base of many salad dressings and is also used as an ingredient in sauces and marinades; as a dip for bread; and for sautéing, roasting, frying and baking. Extra-virgin olive oil can be used as a condiment when drizzled over a bowl of pasta or platter of roasted vegetables. Although olive oil has great health benefits, it also has a lot of calories. It's 100 percent fats, and like all liquid oils, contains about 120 calories per tablespoon.

Olive oil is an excellent source of heart-healthy monounsaturated fats that may lower the bad cholesterol and raise the good cholesterol.

It contains Vitamin E and antioxidants.

It's an excellent replacement for unhealthy saturated fats like butter.

Extra-virgin olive oil has the highest concentration of Vitamin E.

Day 14 High Lights

The "true" you is buried under layers of rejection and conceptual thoughts. Every emotion is an added layer from our false self image or the labeling of others. There are images that we choose not to promote, so we keep them tucked or stored away never to be seen. But what we have stored away is a tiny grain of success waiting to be fed, it has been ignored for so long, we forget of its true potential. However, the more that we exercise it, the more we recognize its strength, resulting in a greater increase in confidence. Improved confidence allows us to make great strides in our personal development. After awhile our confidence grows into a giant, a myriad of characters and traits to project our self image for all to see. Makes no difference what that special thing is, it's yours. You are the originator and rightful owner ready to introduce to the world the best you. Now that you've made it hard to over look; an obvious talent or born trait can now be used to highlight the transformed you and you now enjoy the good life even more. Two weeks in, you're almost there and you're feeling a sense of renewed energy. You are empowered and stronger, and who knows more about highlighting their strengths than R&B singer and songwriter, model and actress Jordan Sparks from Glendale Arizona? She rose to fame as the winner of the sixth season of American Idol as the youngest winner in Idol history at age seventeen.

"You must become your own internal fan. Every moment is for you to be at the top of your game."

~Jordan Sparks

~ You have completed week 2! Awesome! At the end of the book are pages for you to write your reflections for each week that you complete. Talk about how you feel, your energy levels, and add a picture if you like.

Breakfast
Energy Shake
1 ½ c. fresh orange juice
1 banana, frozen, peeled, cut into 2 inch chunks
½ c. coarsely chopped kale leaves, center stalk removed
½ kiwi, peeled
2 pitted dates, coarsely chopped

Midmorning Snack
Spanish Trail Mix
2 cups whole natural almonds
1 ½ t. smoked paprika
1 t. finely grated orange peel
1 c. cubed dried apricots
1 c .cubed pitted dates
½ c .cubed Manchego cheese

Lunch
Fruited Quinoa
¼ c. almond milk
¼ c. water
¼ c. dry quinoa, thoroughly rinsed
½ c. fresh blueberries
¼ t. ground cinnamon
2 t. chopped walnuts, lightly toasted
1 t. brown sugar

Dinner
Lamb Pita Sandwiches w/ Kiwi Yogurt
4 t cumin seeds
¾ t salt
½ t freshly ground black pepper
1 ½ pound trimmed boneless leg of lamb cut into strips
2 ½ T olive oil, divided
1 ¼ c plain Greek style yogurt
2 T chopped fresh cilantro
1 garlic clove, pressed
1 ¼ pounds kiwis, peeled, cubed
4 7 in whole wheat pitas
1 sm. head of romaine lettuce, torn
Hot chili sauce
1 cup thinly sliced red onion

Night Snack
A slice of cantaloupe and handful of almonds

- **Weaknesses** = Unsure results
+ **Strengths** = Dominated ability

Cardio/Workout

Repeat Basic work out w/ circuit training

Crunch & Reach - Begin with body straight over the ball, light weight extended behind you (not shown). Contract the abs to lift and bring the weight over the head, crunching up and twisting to the right, contracting the right side of waist. Repeat for all reps and then switch sides.

Bench Press w/ dumb bells

Bike or Job

The Health Benefits of Citrus

We all know citrus fruits are loaded with vitamin C; one orange has a whole day's requirement. But that's not all citrus fruits have to offer.

Citrus juice contains flavonoids, a phytonutrient that lowers the body's production of cholesterol, inhibits blood clot formation and boosts the bang of vitamin C.

They're also loaded with soluble fiber which lowers cholesterol, maintains healthy blood sugar levels and helps you to manage your weight.

That explosion of scent that erupts when you grate a citrus peel is produced by limonene, oil found in the peel that might inhibit a variety of cancers.

Oranges and grapefruits are in peak season during the winter. Their bright flavors are a perfect antidote to a cold,

Day 15 ~ Force

Whether consciously or not we practice a number of unhealthy thoughts that create self-doubt. When this occurs, our thoughts of "what might be" are never even transmitted to the brain. There is a great divide that prevents positive thinking from impacting critical change. And, like most of the phenomenal events that happen in life the process of change is not always easy. Take the birth of mankind. The baby does not just suddenly appear; she must be pushed out. Sometimes, so forcefully to bypass whatever is in her path. If you are really expecting to complete this Life plan successfully, be prepared to push through the trials and tribulations that may seem at times impossible to move. You have to take on this change process not afraid to use force if necessary. Who else knows about force better than Martial artist, Michael Jay White who holds seven black belts? White started training at age of seven, earning a reputation as a fearsomely tough street fighter by the age of fourteen. Unsure of what direction to take in life, White became a junior high school teacher specializing in emotionally disturbed children. Your path may not be what you expect it to be, but take your destiny by force and become what is great inside of you.

"Work through whatever needs to be done, no matter how you feel. Intimidation must take a back seat. Force is your only option."
~ Michael Jay White

Breakfast
Energy Shake
1 ½ c. fresh orange juice
1 banana, frozen, peeled, cut into 2 inch chunks
½ c. coarsely chopped kale leaves, center stalk removed
½ kiwi, peeled
2 pitted dates, coarsely chopped

Midmorning Snack
½ cup of almonds
½ c dried mango, chopped
½ c dried cranberries

Lunch
Chicken Wrap with Salad
1 whole wheat tortilla
6 oz. Skinless chicken breast
½ cup of black beans
½ cup pico de gallo
2 cups mixed green salad w/ fresh tangerines

Dinner
Grilled Tilapia with Fennel- Mint Tzatziki
  ½ cup of finely diced fennel bulb
  ½ cup Greek style yogurt
  ¾ T chopped fresh mint
  ½ t white balsamic vinegar
  2 T extra virgin olive oil (EVOO)
  2 large tilapia fillets
  ½ t fennel seeds, finely ground
  1 cup of Broccoli with lemon and 1 T olive oil

Night Snack
½ c strawberry sorbet with ¼ cup of fresh blueberries

- **Friction** = To interfere or hinder with personal currency

+ **Flow** = A fluent station of uninterrupted power

Stretching & Breathing

Add to Stretching & Breathing Model

Warrior II - This pose enables energy to flow through your limbs and inspires courage and wisdom. Facing the front of your mat with your feet hip-width apart, step your left foot forward and your right foot back, turning it slightly at an angle. Bend your front knee so that your thigh is parallel to the floor and your knee is directly over your ankle. Lift your arms to shoulder height, in line with your body. Inhale and exhale deeply as you gaze toward your front hand. As you press your feet into the mat, make it your intention to draw them in toward each other, to engage your inner thigh muscles. Expand your inner thighs and sitting bones back and apart as you root down through your tailbone, extending out through your legs and arms. Lengthen your torso upward. Repeat on the opposite side. Hold for 3 to 5 deep breaths.

The Health Benefits of Whole Grains

Look for grains in their least processed form, and try to eat them every day. Some immediate benefits you might notice are stable blood sugar, less hunger between meals and better weight management. Sure, whole grains can sometimes take a little longer to prepare than their quick and instant counterparts, but the benefits and flavor of whole grain are worth the extra effort.

They are delicious, inexpensive and packed with protein, B vitamins, minerals and fiber.

Grains contain many of the same antioxidants found in fruits and vegetables.

Research shows a diet high in whole grains may help prevent heart disease, some cancers, obesity and diabetes.

Day 16 ~ Ghost

We name this chapter Ghost, short for "give up the ghost." A ghost is relevant to being in hiding, as we are when we feel shame or exiled from the world. The truth is, if the ghost did such a good job hiding then its description would have never been reported. Our condition is very similar in that before we "give up the ghost," we think we are hiding, but mostly everyone sees what we are going through, because as ghosts we are transparent and distant. *This chapter is devoted to being true to self.* And that's exactly what Caryn Elane Johnson would have to do after dropping out of high school and becoming addicted to heroin. She moved to California and established the San Diego Repertory. She would later be introduced to the world as Whoopi Goldberg. When giving up old behavior you must be careful in not losing your original drive. Unhealthy substances could stop us from accomplishing our goals, but we must not give the substance that much credit. Remember your committed behavior to support the addiction was influenced by our original character. Use that same commitment to push through these last days of discovering a healthier, new you.

Breakfast
½ c. of Dried Blueberries
1 cup oat meal

Midmorning Snack
½ c Greek yogurt with 3 T. granola
Handful of almonds

Lunch
Chicken Salad Pita
3 oz. boneless, skinless chicken breast
½ apple, small –
1 tbsp. diced celery
1/8 cup pineapple chunks
1/8 cup grape halves
½ whole wheat pita pocket (6-inch diameter)
1 romaine lettuce leaf
1 tbsp. light mayonnaise/veganaise

Dinner
Spicy Shrimp Quesadillas
    12 large shrimp, grilled and coarsely chopped
    2 T chopped fresh cilantro + additional for garnish
    3 jalapenos, seeded and thinly sliced
    2 T chopped shallot
    1 T fresh lime juice
    2 c coarsely grated Jack cheese
    8 7 to 8 inch whole wheat tortillas
    8 teaspoons EVOO

Night Snack
½ c granola with dried cherries

- Natural = Where your ability can be inverted or rejected

+ Supernatural = Where your ability is not subject to the laws of nature and exists above and beyond

Cardio/Workout

Repeat Basic work out w/ circuit training

Bicycles - Pull knees up towards chest and push legs outward

Triceps Extension - Hold weight ball or light weights over your head and bring down to your chest

Squats - Level arms out and bend legs as you lower your body

The Health Benefits of Berries

All fruits are stellar sources of nutrients, but strawberries, raspberries, blueberries and blackberries stand out from the pack.

They're high in vitamin and fiber content.

They're an excellent source of antioxidants, compounds that protect our bodies from the stress of day to day living. The antioxidant anthocyanin has tripled the stress-fighting power of vitamin C and is known to block cancer-causing damage as well as the effects of many age-related diseases.

They give your memory a boost. The antioxidants in berries are believed to enhance brain function.

Fresh berries are kind to the waistline; they are naturally high in water and low in calories. Dried berries also provide excellent nutrition, but since most of the water is missing, their calories are more concentrated and you'll usually wind up eating more of them.

Stock up on fresh berries in the summer, when they're plentiful and inexpensive. Freeze them in small plastic bags to get an antioxidant blast year round.

| Motivation | Meal Plan |

Day 17 Crucifixion

Crucifixion- (James/Allen)

In order to enjoy life we must die to self. A British Philosophical writer known for his inspirational books. From one of his most popular writings, *As a Man Thinketh* he wrote that "men are unwilling to improve themselves; therefore, they must remain bound. The man who does not shrink from self-crucifixion can never fail to accomplish the object which upon his heart is set". A lot of times we look high and low to what could be causing the problems in our lives. My suggestion? Try removing the old self.

Day 17 Activity

Exercise- Make a list of all the things you want gone from your old behavior, bury it with a witness present, and then have a celebration of new beginnings with your closest friends or support group.

Breakfast
Berry Energy Shake
1 banana, frozen, peeled, and sliced
½ cup fresh or frozen blackberries
½ cup fresh or frozen blueberries
2 packets Stevia Extract In The Raw
½ cup light vanilla soymilk or almond milk

Midmorning Snack
½ c. granola with ½ c. dried cherries

Lunch
Tuna Wraps
1 T olive oil
2 medium plum tomatoes, seeded, finely chopped
1 medium onion, finely chopped
2 garlic cloves
1 pound high quality tuna packed in olive oil
2 large hard boiled eggs, peeled, sliced
1 pkg. whole wheat flat bread
Lettuce of choice

Dinner
Grilled Open Face Eggplant and Smoked Gouda
1 lb. Tomatoes, finely chopped
¼ c. finely chopped fresh flat leaf parsley
½ c plus 2 T. EVOO
1 T. white wine vinegar
½ t. black pepper
1 t. Kosher Salt
1- 8 oz. Piece smoked cheese (gouda)
4 slices whole grain bread
2-1 lb. Eggplants

Night Snack
½ c. Greek yogurt with ½ c blueberries

- **Death** = the continuation of destruction

+ **Rebirth** = A new mindset to overcome debilitating habits

Stretching & Breathing

Seven (7) don'ts after a meal

Add to Stretching & Breathing Model

Bridge (Feb 2010 Natural Health Magazine) This pose expands the area around your heart and lungs, allowing you to take deeper breaths and open up to the possibilities of joy. Lying on your back, bend your knees and place your feet hip-width apart. Keeping your arms alongside your body, bend your elbows and point your fingers upward. Inhale, ground your feet and lift your hips to come into a backbend. As you exhale, lower your arms and clasp them under your body. Keep the sides of your body long and your throat open. Bring your shoulder blades down your back as you begin to feel your chest open, unleashing your natural joy. Hold to 3 to 5 breaths.

~ Don't smoke- experiments from experts prove that smoking a cigarette after a meal is comparable to smoking cigarettes (chances of cancer are higher)

~ Don't eat fruit immediately- Immediately eating fruits after meals will cause stomach to be bloated with air. Therefore, take fruit 1-2 hours after meal or 1 hour before meal.

~ Don't drink tea- Because tea leaves contain a high content of acid. This substance will cause the protein content in the food we consume to harden thus difficult to digest.

~ Don't loosen your belt- Loosening the belt after a meal will easily cause the intestine to be twisted and blocked.

~ Don't bathe- Bathing will cause the increase of blood flow to the hands, legs and body, thus the amount of blood around the stomach will therefore decrease. This will weaken the digestive system in our stomach.

~ Don't walk about- People always say that after a meal walk a hundred steps and you will live till 99. In actual fact this is not true. Walking will cause the digestive system to be unable to absorb

Day 18 Dimension

It is said that somewhere within the dimensions of your life, you are destined to perform better than, as expected, or worse than what destiny has written for you. The goal is to mentally align your dimension with your desires so that you live out the dreams and visions that you have seen. I'm sure many of us would enjoy creating a mechanism that appears when we are in danger. Let's take the creator of the original Green lantern, a young struggling artist Martin Nodell who was born in Philadelphia, Pennsylvania. He first worked as a freelance writer when he began to quantum leap into a dimension that defined his purpose by implementing the imagination of his fictitious character. The Green lantern yields a power ring that can generate a variety of effects, sustained purely by the ring wearers imagination and strength of will. The greater the users will power, the more effective the ring. If you are not impressed with what is currently taking place in your lives, you should change it. Your life can really be that manageable with the reconstruction of our thoughts. These things may not appear as sudden as it did so for The Green Lantern, but with time we can create what's needed to guide us where we are going in life. Whether we wear a ring or bracelet to remind us of our victories in change, remember our rightful dimension is out there somewhere in the universe.

Breakfast
Berry Energy Shake
1 banana, frozen, peeled, and sliced
½ cup fresh or frozen blackberries
½ cup fresh or frozen blueberries
2 packets Stevia Extract In The Raw
½ cup light vanilla soymilk or almond milk

Midmorning Snack
Banana with 2 T. peanut butter
8 oz. Almond milk

Lunch
Grilled Hearts of Romaine with Blue Cheese Vinaigrette and Pickled Onions
1 ¾ c white wine vinegar, divided
½ c. sugar
½ c water
3 Turkish bay leaves
½ t crushed red pepper
1 to 1 ¼ lbs red onions sliced thinly
½ t Dijon mustard
½ c olive oil
½ c crumbled blue cheese
4 hearts of romaine, quartered
Crumbled blue cheese, for garnish

Dinner
Grilled Chicken Breast w/ Orange Pineapple Chutney
4 boneless/skinless chicken breast or thighs
1 ½ navel oranges
1 golden delicious apple, peeled, cored, cubed
½ red onion, coarsely chopped
1/3 cup fresh cilantro
1 T chopped/seeded jalapeno
1 T evoo
1 T red wine vinegar
1 T agave nectar/honey (orange blossom is great!)
1 t of garam masala
1 t minced peeled fresh ginger
Serve with ½ cup of brown rice per serving

Night Snack
½ c. granola and 1 banana

- **Astray** = Settling, unfulfilled goals come from incomplete thoughts; drifting into cyber space from lack of belief to produce a complete version.
+ **Alignment** = Align your thoughts and ideas with the resources to bring it to life.

Cardio/Workout

Good heart snacks

Repeat Basic work out w/ circuit training

It is more beneficial for the heart if you eat meals regularly, rather than the traditional three meals a day. This is especially true of a heavy dinner which exerts additional pressure on the heart to supply the rest of the body with the nutrients it needs. Good snacks include:

A.

B.

C.

Reverse Crunch

Stewed apples and blackberries
Grapefruit and orange-segment fruit salad
Avocado dip on rye cakes
Tahini(sesame seed dip) on oatcakes
Sardines on ryvita
Salmon on buckwheat blinis
Spinach salad with pine nuts
Tuna and sweet corn salad
Lentil and carrot soup
Mixed vegetables and barley soup

Military Press

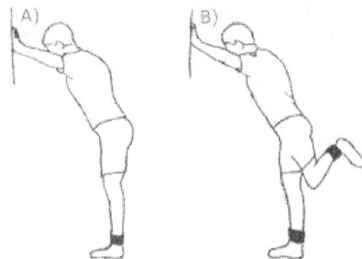

Leg Curls

Day 19 ~ Self Principles

"Do not do onto others what you do not want done to yourself"
    ~ Confucius

Some of us treat others better than we do ourselves. We have integrity and give more thought when it comes to our concern for others, usually following the concepts of a teaching that put emphasis as how to treat thy neighbor but run short of its principle when it comes to self. Confucius practiced techniques that empowered self. His teachings later turned into an elaborate set of rules and practices organized into the Analects. These teachings are still followed today.

Day 19 Post-Activity Plan

Earlier on day 6 you were asked to create a set of life principles to live by as a guide book to the new you. The idea now is to reflect and evaluate the progress that you have made since developing self principles. Be specific on your dos and don'ts and highlight your levels of growth based off the 13 day comparison.

Breakfast
½ c. of Dried Blueberries
1 banana
1 cup oat meal

Midmorning Snack
1 medium orange and handful of almonds

Lunch
Grilled Shrimp, Lettuce, and Cherry Tomato Salad with Aioli Dressing
5 oz. Blackened shrimp
12 cups torn romaine lettuce from 1 large head
8 oz cherry tomatoes
1 garlic clove, pressed
3 T. light mayonnaise/veganaise
1 ½ T. white wine vinegar

Dinner
Mixed Greens with Pears, Walnuts, Gorgonzola and Green Tea Vinaigrette
2 T. Champagne vinegar
1 T. minced shallot
1 T. chopped fresh chives
2 t. Dijon mustard
1 t. dried basil
1 t. matcha green-tea powder
6 T. EVOO
6 c. loosely packed mixed greens
2 pears, peeled, halved lengthwise, cut into ½ inch wedges
½ c. crumbled Gorgonzola cheese

Night Snack
2 celery stalks, 2 T. peanut butter and raisins

- Rules = A system of guidelines that's favored by majority
+ Principles = Internal laws that you live by and never forsake

Stretching & Breathing

Add to Stretching & Breathing Model

Cat Stretch – These are great for the lower back muscles and ligaments. Kneel on the floor and place and place your hands in front of you (on the floor) about shoulder length apart. Relax your trunk and lower back. Now arch the spine and pull in your abdomen as far as you can and hold this position for a few seconds. Repeat the exercise 4 to 5 times.

The Cholesterol Connection

Cholesterol 20 years ago was thought to be the major cause of heart disease. Although it is certainly a contributory factor, it is important to remember that our bodies actually need and manufacture cholesterol every day for vital functions. Cholesterol is a naturally occurring substance in the body, produced by the liver in varying quantities (but usually less than 3 grams per day). It is used in membranes and for the formation of hormones; it is required for the synthesis of vitamin D, and in the nervous system it is a constituent of the myelin sheath, the protective covering on all nerves. Usually, any excess cholesterol in the body binds with fibre and is excreted via the bowels. However, if large amounts accumulate, they can cause the formation of gallstones, or may be stored as fat in cellulite, or seen as small white or yellowish spots just below the eyes.

There are two types of cholesterol: high-density lipoprotein (HDL) and low-density lipoprotein (LDL). The two balance each other. The HDL removes cholesterol from vulnerable areas, taking it back to the liver for recycling and disposal, while the LDL does the opposite- it delivers cholesterol throughout the body to where it is required. Both are carried in the blood.

Motivation

Day 20 Creation

Creation (mad scientist)

Your presence is the light switch to life. When you walk into a room, it's your energy that sets the environment. Most of your situations and circumstances are all created by your thoughts. Many of us give praise or acknowledgement to a higher power of a creator, but lack or reject the responsibilities as co-creator and offspring of His power. The Koran quotes "The thought was the cause of it all". The Bible states "Life and death is in the power of the tongue". Let's face it, our tongue is an instrument that interprets what we believe in, that speaks based on what we think. In essence we are fragments of the things we think of and our spoken ideologies are prerecorded. We think it; say it and it comes to life. "So as a man thinketh so is he". "It's Alive!" a famous quote that became popular in the 1931 classic, Frankenstein scene where Colin Clive goes insane as the monster comes to life. We are the monster that we create, as well as the scientist that explores and enjoys life. So, it is important to speak of the things we want and keep the complaints and unwanted things to a minimum, realizing that you are the creator of your outcome.

Create something fabulous today!!

Meal Plan

Breakfast
Energy Shake
1 ½ c. fresh orange juice
1 banana, frozen, peeled, cut into 2 inch chunks
½ c. coarsely chopped kale leaves, center stalk removed
½ kiwi, peeled
2 pitted dates, coarsely chopped

Midmorning Snack
½ c granola and raisins ¼ c dark chocolate chips

Lunch
Beef and Lettuce Wraps
Hearts of Romaine
8 oz sirloin steak or veggie steak strips
2 cups of zucchini
½ c. sliced red onion
1 cup of brown rice
2 t. Dijon vinaigrette

Dinner
Grilled Tilapia with Fennel- Mint Tzatziki
½ cup of finely diced fennel bulb
½ cup Greek style yogurt
¾ T chopped fresh mint
½ t white balsamic vinegar
2 T extra virgin olive oil (EVOO)
2 large tilapia fillets
½ t fennel seeds, finely ground
1 cup of Broccoli with lemon and 1 T. olive oil

Night Snack
½ c almonds and dried cranberries
½ c mandarin oranges

- **Stress** = Unhealthy thoughts block healthy thoughts.
+ **Peace** = All creation derived from our thoughts, but only when our thoughts are at peace should we create.

Cardio/Workout

Repeat Basic work out with circuit training

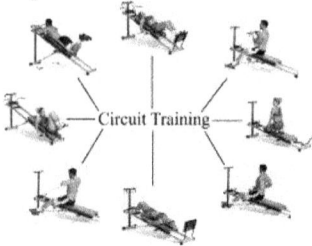

Circuit Training

Gym or Home
Do a thorough evaluation and see if you are on the right path to completing your goal!

Pre-Test	Post-Test

Cardio respiratory Endurance
1.5 Mile Run   Time _:_
1.0 Mile Walk Time_:_
       Heart Rate_:_
	Cardio respiratory Endurance
	1.5 Mile Run Time _:_
	1.0 Mile Walk Time_:_
	       Heart Rate_:_

Muscular strength/endurance *Reps* Modified Push-Ups ___ Abs Crunches ___ Overall Fitness Category ___	Muscular strength/endurance *Reps* Modified Push-Ups ___ Abs Crunches ___ Overall Fitness Category ___
Flexibility Modified Sit-and-Reach *Inches* ____	Flexibility Modified Sit-and-Reach *Inches* ____
BMI/body composition Current body weight ___lbs Current fat percent ___% Waist seize ___Inches	BMI/body composition Current body weight ___lbs Current fat percent ___% Waist seize ___Inches

Compare results

Brown Power

Brown Rice
Brown rice has 3 more grams of fiber per serving than white rice, so I stick with the darker option whenever possible. It's especially good if you're rolling some homemade sushi.

Natural Peanut Butter
Most processed peanut butter like you'll find at the grocery store are stuffed with added sugars and other junk that take away from this food's natural goodness. Stay away from those, and instead opt for the natural kind, which is high in fiber and protein. Want a great sweet tooth remedy? Try a natty PB and Banana sandwich on whole wheat bread.

Walnuts
Walnuts are another great source of Omega-3's, and are also packed with Vitamin E - a powerful antioxidant that can help your muscles recovery from tough gym sessions. They make a great addition to oatmeal and shakes, but are also delicious on their lonesome.

Day 21 Cycle

Cycle (Cocoon) a 1985 Science Fiction Film Laws, order to life

In this Ron Howard production, there is a pool which causes people to feel younger and happier again. The ending shows most of them return with the Aliens to a place where they will never grow ill, never age, and never die. I often thought about this concept of "what if", especially as I got older and had been through a series of events. But it was those events that led me to becoming a motivational speaker and inspired me to write this book. Many of us would agree that there would not be a benefit to the future, if the next generation didn't learn from the flaws and mistakes that we make in life. We are educated by those individuals who have used these practices in their own lives, and are now instructors of its great endeavors. We may not be able to postpone our age, but we can remain as young as we feel by the information provided by the ones before us. Such is the nature of using The Black Out Life Plan. Apple seed equals apple tree, and after the development of the tree each apple produces the equivalent ability to create its own tree. The same applies for each of your attributes that have been strengthened within this 21 day process. Not only do you as an individual stand tall in symbolic reference as the tree, but you too have the ability to grow and branch out to others. So, even if you lived forever the true fountain of your youth would be offering others a healthier and prosperous lifestyle that all can enjoy. It's ok to repeat this 21 day process as much as necessary. Your success is based on your determination, will, desire, and persistence.
GO GET IT!!!!

Breakfast
Mushroom & Spinach Frittata with Roasted Tomatoes
1-10.5 oz container grape tomatoes
¾ c diced shallots, divided
1 t. evoo
12 oz. Mushrooms (crimini/stemmed shitake), diced
1 c fresh baby spinach, wilted
2 ½ T chopped fresh basil, divided
6 large eggs
1 T Dijon mustard
1/3 c crumbled fresh goat cheese
Splash of balsamic vinegar

Midmorning Snack
½ c granola with dried cherries

Lunch
Beet and Tangerine Salad w/ Cranberry Dressing
3- 2 ½ in diameter red beets, tops trimmed
3 large tangerines
3 T. evoo
3 T. frozen cranberry juice cocktail, thawed
1 T raspberry vinegar
1/3 c paper thin slices red onion
1 large bunch watercress, thick stems trimmed
1 boneless skinless chicken breast, grilled, sliced

Dinner
Lamb Pita Sandwiches w/ Kiwi Yogurt
4 t cumin seeds
¾ t salt
½ t freshly ground black pepper
1 ½ pound trimmed boneless leg of lamb cut into strips
2 ½ T olive oil, divided
1 ¼ c plain Greek style yogurt
2 T chopped fresh cilantro
1 garlic clove, pressed
1 ¼ pounds kiwis, peeled, cubed
4 7 in whole wheat pitas
1 sm. head of romaine lettuce, torn
Hot chili sauce
1 cup thinly sliced red onion

Night Snack
½ cup fruit sorbet and handful of almonds

- Insanity = to repeat the same thing and expect different results
+ Destiny = to define ones purpose and outcome

Stretching & Breathing

Add to Stretching & Breathing Model

Full-Body Stretch - **End your practice with this expansive, soothing and stress-releasing stretch.** Bring your legs slightly apart and extend your arms alongside your ears. Reach out evenly through the heels and balls of your feet, spread your toes, and stretch strongly up through your torso and out through your arms and fingers. Imagine a light shining out through your heart with a spirit of celebrating love. To release, lower your arms to your sides (slightly away from your body), breathe deeply and relax here for 5 minutes.

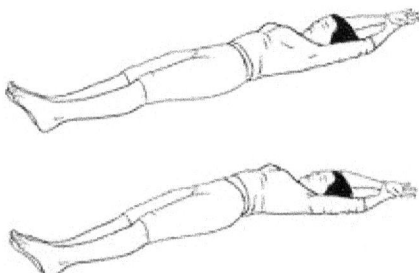

~ You have completed 21 days to creating a new you! Awesome! At the end of the book are pages for you to write your reflections for each week that you complete. Talk about how you feel, your energy levels, and add a picture if you like. Look at how much you have accomplished. You should be so very proud of yourself. I am!

Starch Intake

Limiting the amount of sugar and starchy foods you consume can help you lose weight as long as you are eating a healthy, well-balanced diet at the same time. You shouldn't completely eliminate healthy starches from your diet, according to the Dietary Guidelines for Americans. These include whole grains, fruit and vegetables. However, eliminating processed sugars and starches from your diet can help you achieve 1,500 calories per day while still getting the vitamins and nutrients necessary to maintain good health.

Meat

Fresh meat is free from sugars and starches. Lean meats, like chicken, fish and turkey, are the best choices for keeping the calories low. Fatty meats like beef and pork contain additional calories from the fat content.

Reflections of ME – Week 1

Reflections of ME – Week 2

Reflections of ME – Week 3

www.ingramcontent.com/pod-product-compliance
Lightning Source LLC
Chambersburg PA
CBHW071745020426
42331CB00008B/2189